Early Jewish Liturgy:

A Sourcebook for use by students of Early Christian Liturgy

edited and translated by

Alistair Stewart-Sykes and Judith H Newman

GROVE BOOKS LIMITED

RIDLEY HALL RD CAMBRIDGE CB3 9HU

Contents

THE EDITORS

Alistair Stewart-Sykes is Vicar of Sturminster Marshall, Kingston Lacy and Shapwick
Judith H. Newman is Associate Professor of Old Testament Studies at the General Theological Seminary, New York

THE COVER PICTURE
is taken from the Nash papyrus of the ten commandments with the shema immediately following, as reproduced in F C Burkitt, 'The Hebrew Papyrus of the Ten Commandments' in JQR 15 (1903), and is reprinted here by permission of the Syndics of Cambridge University Library.

First Impression December 2001
ISSN 0951-2667
ISBN 1 85174 486 X

Preface

The aim of this volume

The statement that Christian liturgy was a derivative of Jewish liturgy, which was once a statement of the obvious, is now a statement beset with difficulty. The task of reconstructing the liturgy of Judaism from the sources which we possess is analogous to that of reconstructing English mediaeval liturgy equipped with Cosin's *Durham Book*, the Victorian worship regulation acts, a secondary (and apologetic) work from a later period such as the *Parson's Handbook*, and a few stray comments in contemporary works such as the *Paston Letters*. Anyone familiar with the field would recognize that the rough equivalents of these sources are the Mishnah, the Tosefta, the Babylonian Talmud and the works of Philo and Josephus, and would recognize further that the developments within Judaism in the first two centuries of the common era are potentially as great as those taking place in English Christianity as a result of the Reformation. In addition to the problem posed by the relative lateness and paucity of the sources, we must recognize that liturgy was not codified either in early Christianity or early Judaism, and so the sources given here are not actually liturgical books. As a result, any liturgical information must be gleaned from between the lines. Further difficulties are posed by the fact that any source which we have may reflect solely the practice of one, perhaps eccentric, group, and that both religions were made up of a variety of such groups; the variety in both groups was so great that to talk of either as a single phenomenon is dangerously anachronistic. Similarly, when dealing with the rabbinic evidence, we should be aware of extrapolating widespread practice from the opinion or practice of one rabbi alone.

Thus, whereas in the past it was possible to make assumptions about the derivation of Christian practices from those of Judaism, nowadays the assumptions which underlie those early works seem facile in the extreme. On the other hand, there is no doubt that many early Christians were Jewish and that Jewish contexts were among the contexts in which early forms of Christianity grew up. Thus, when we are confronted by a clear parallel of practice deriving from a Christian context in which a relationship to Judaism is demonstrable, such as when the Didache, which is of a demonstrably Jewish Christian background, states that baptism is to be performed, by preference, in 'living water', we may be justified, in view of the startling similarity with the Jewish injunctions contained in Mishnah *Mikwaoth* 1.8, in claiming that there is a relationship between the practices.

It is in the light of these comments that the aim of the editors of this volume is to be understood. That is to say, our task is to present the reader whose principal interest is in Christian liturgy, and who may well be prone to confusion and bewilderment when faced with the Jewish material, with the available evidence from Jewish sources in a readily accessible format. The evidence chosen for presentation is selected either because, in the opinion of the editors, there is some connection with Christian practice or because such a connection has been claimed by others in the past. No distinction between these classes of material is made in the arrangement, which is primarily thematic. This is by no means a complete sourcebook for the study of early Jewish liturgy for its own sake, as the selections are made solely with a mind to the possibility of a relationship with early Christian liturgy and as a means of understanding the development of liturgy in early Christianity. Comments are added to each citation by way of guidance, in particular to suggest the possible way in which the material is related to Christian liturgy, and to introduce the student to the debate. Christian sources are not included, as it is assumed that the reader has a ready understanding of, and access to, these sources. The criteria for selection mean the exclusion of much material relating to Jewish liturgy, and it must be clearly understood that, whilst the editors are indebted greatly to the labours of scholars in the field of Jewish liturgy, that is not the field in which this work belongs. Even less is it a contribution to the study of the documents which are excerpted here.

The Sources
The Jewish sources which are employed in this work are as follow:
1) The Dead Sea Scrolls: Found at Qumran, near the Dead Sea, in the middle of the last century, these documents illustrate forms of Judaism as they were before the destruction of the Temple. Citation is by number, the first of which is the number of the cave in which the relevant fragment was found.
2) Josephus: Josephus was a Jewish historian of the first century of the common era; originating in Palestine, he ended his life in Rome, which was the location of his literary career.
3) Philo: Philo was an Alexandrian Jewish teacher of the first century of the common era.
4) The Mishnah: The Mishnah is a codification of Jewish law as it was understood at the beginning of the third century. It was produced in Babylonia, and takes the form of a series of opinions on various topics. The topics, around which it is organised, and according to which it is cited, are known as tractates. Thus, for instance, the tractate *Pesahim* deals with laws surrounding the conduct of the Passover (*Pesah*).
5) The Tosefta: This is a supplement to the Mishnah from the end of the third century, arranged along the tractates of the Mishnah. It adds additional directions to those contained in the Mishnah, both adding detail to the regulations of the Mishnah and codifying additional regulations. [1]

---

1   Because of the diversity among the texts, it should be noted that all translations from the Tosefta are taken from *The Tosefta According to the Codex Vienna, with variants from Codes Erfurt, Genizah MSS and Editio Princeps (Venice 1521) Together with references to parallel passages in Talmudic Literature* (Jewish Theological Seminary, Jerusalem, 1992-1995).

4

6) The Talmuds: There are two Talmuds, from Babylon and Palestine; both are massive commentaries on the Mishnah, and are arranged along the tractates of the Mishnah. It is important to note that all the rabbinic material cites debate and argument, but this is particularly true of the Talmuds.

In addition, material of a fragmentary nature is employed from a variety of sources, whose origin is explained in the comment on each.

As was hinted earlier in this introduction, Judaism underwent change in the first centuries of the common era, as did Christianity, and therefore the later sources must be used with the greatest of caution in discussing Christian practice. We hope that, apart from making these sources available, we demonstrate the proper caution which is to be shown in the use of this material.

The authors

Since the work bears the name of two authors, the reader should be aware of the division of responsibility, and therefore of blame. The bulk of the translation is the work of Dr Newman, who is responsible for all translations from Hebrew and Aramaic, with the exceptions of the passages from the Mishnah and the Dead Sea Scrolls, whereas Dr Stewart-Sykes is responsible for the selection of material, for the comments, and for the remainder of the translation.

1
The *birkath haMinim* and the parting of the ways

The *Birkath haMinim*, or benediction against heretics, formed one of the benedictions of the *tefillah*, which was one of the basic components of the prayer of the synagogue from at least the first century. The date of this particular benediction is however less certain, as is its applicability to Christians. The following text of the prayer is, found among the texts discovered in the Cairo genizah.[2]

1) For apostates let there be no hope, and speedily root out the dominion of arrogance in our days; and let Christians (*nozrim*) and heretics (*minim*) perish in a moment, let them be blotted out of the book of the living for ever and not be written with the righteous. Blessed are you, Lord, who humble the insolent.

(Cairo Genizah text)

On the origin of this benediction the Talmud has the following:

2) Are these eighteen really nineteen? R. Levi said: 'The benediction of the *Minim*[3] was established in Yabneh.' According to what was it to correspond? R. Levi said: 'In the view of R. Hillel the son of R. Samuel bar Nahmani, to "The God of Glory thunders"; in the view of R. Joseph, to "the word 'one' that is proclaimed in the *Shema*"; in the view of R. Tanhum quoting R. Joshua b. Levi, "according to the little vertebrae in the spine".'

Our Rabbis taught: 'Simeon haPakuli ordered the eighteen benedictions before Rab Gamaliel in Yabneh. He said to the Sages: "Can any one among you compose a benediction concerning the *Minim*?" Samuel the Lesser stood up and composed it. The next year he forgot it and tried for two or three hours to remember it, but they did not remove him.'

Why did they not remove him seeing that Rab Judah said in the name of Rab: "In the case of all the other benedictions, no one is removed [for making a mistake], but if [a mistake is made] in the benediction of the *Minim*, he is to be removed, because we consider him a *Min*"? Samuel the Lesser who composed it is different.'

(BT *Berakoth* 28B-29A)

There is no certainty that Christians are particularly intended by the benediction as described here, rather any divergent form of Judaism from that

---

2   The Cairo Genizah was a mediaeval Jewish library discovered late in the nineteenth century. The text translated here was published by S Schechter, 'Genizah specimens' in *JQR* 10 (1897-1898), 656-657.

3   The Soncino edition of the Babylonian Talmud adopts manuscript editions that contain *birkat haZaddukim*, ('blessing of the righteous ones') the equivalent of a subjective genitive, referring presumably to the Rabbis who were responsible for composing the blessing, rather than using the objective genitive *birkat haMinim* ('blessing of the heretics').

being established at Yabneh was to be excluded. The explanation attributed to Rab that a *min* would convict himself by failing to read the benediction is, however, hardly convincing, because a diverging Jew would not consider himself divergent. The prayer does exhibit the context in which Judaism and Christianity were set to separate, even if it is not originally intended specifically to exclude Christians, or excluded Jewish Christians only, and Christians might well consider that the benediction was intended against them. Thus Justin, at *Dialogue* 16, 47 and 96, states that Christians are cursed in the synagogues.

The break with Judaism was not, however entirely clean. The following is recorded from the late second century:

3] Was it not taught that Rab stated: 'Why use the Syriac language in *Eretz Israel?* . . . either the holy tongue or the Greek language.' R. Yosei of Babylon said: 'Why use the Aramaic language? . . . either the holy tongue or the Persian language.'

(BT *Baba Qamma* 82B-83A)

That Syriac was banned from sacred use is an indication of some missionary activity among Jews in Syria. The point which is gathered from this discussion is that the relationship between Christians and Jews, whilst always tense, was complex because of the extent to which they shared common ground. In examining the topic of the manner in which early Jewish and early Christian liturgy developed, it is important to realize that both were in the process of development from a common origin, and that it is possible for development to take place in either one with an eye on the other. The attitude to *minim* and their tables, whilst not necessarily denoting Christianity, would seem to fit Christians well enough, and Jewish Christians especially:

4) The act of slaughter of a *min* [is] idolatry.
Their bread is the bread of a Samaritan, and their wine is considered wine used for idolatrous purposes, and their produce is deemed wholly untithed and their books are decreed magical books and their children are *mamzerin*.
People should not sell anything to them or buy anything from them. And they should not take wives from them or give children in marriage to them. And they should not teach their sons a craft. And they should not seek help from them, either financial or medical.

(Tosefta *Hullin* 2.20)

Further reading:
R Kimelman, '*Birkat Ha-Minim* and the Lack of Evidence for an Anti-Christian Jewish Prayer in Late Antiquity' in E P Sanders *et al.* (edd.) *Jewish and Christian Self-Definition* II (Fortress, Philadelphia PA, 1981)
W Horbury, 'The benediction of the *minim* and early Jewish Christian controversy' in *JTS* (ns) 33 (1982), 19-61

2
The synagogue and the church as forming institutions

The primary purpose of the synagogue, whilst the Temple was still standing, was that of the study of the law and Scriptures, though in the diaspora it might also function as something of a cultural centre. The following account of the activity of an Alexandrian synagogue is left by Philo:

5) On these seventh days, he [Moses] required them to assemble in the same place and to sit with one another with decency and good order to listen to the laws so that nobody should be ignorant. And thus they always assemble and sit together with each other. They do so for the most part in silence except when it is thought proper to add something to that which is being read. One of the priests who is present, or one of the elders, reads the laws to them and interprets them point by point until late in the afternoon. And then they depart, having gained profound understanding of the sacred laws and having advanced greatly in piety.

(Philo *Apology* 7.12-13)

6) Thus there stand open, each seventh day, thousands of schools of understanding, temperance, bravery, justice and the other virtues, in every city. In them people sit in good order in quiet and with ears alert, with undivided attention on account of their thirst for the verbal drink, whilst one of special experience stands up and expounds those things which are best and most profitable, and which tend to give improvement to the whole of life.

(Philo *On the special laws* 2.62)

In a fictive address put into the mouth of an opponent of Jewish practice, Philo characterizes the activities of the Sabbath thus:

7) And will you sit in your gatherings, and repair to your regular company, and read your sacred books in security, conversing over any point of obscurity, and discussing at leisurely length your ancestral philosophy?

(Philo *On dreams* 12.127)

The same was true in Palestine:

8) He [Moses] appointed the law as the most excellent and necessary means of instruction, ordering that it should be heard not once, or twice, or occasionally, but that each week, deserting their other duties, men should gather to listen to the law, and thus should gain a thorough and accurate knowledge.

(Josephus *Against Apion* 2.175)

And, if the fictive setting of the speech from which the extract below is to be believed, it was also true in Greece:

9) We give over the seventh day to learning our customs and law.

(Josephus *Jewish Antiquities* 16.43)

Because of this fundamentally intellectual activity there was a close relationship between the synagogue as a house of assembly and the schools, as described in this conversation.

10) It happened that R Yohanan ben Beroqah and R Eleazar b Chisma came from Yabneh to Lud and they greeted R Joshua in Peqi'in. R Joshua said to them: 'What was new in the house of study [*beit haMidrash*] today?' They said to him 'We are your students and we drink your water.' He said to them: 'It is impossible that there should be nothing new in the house of study today. Whose Sabbath was it?' They said to him: 'It was the Sabbath of R Eleazar ben Azariah.' He said to them 'And how did he expound?' 'Assemble the people, the men, the women and the children.' 'If men come to study, women come to listen, why do children come?' 'To provide a reward to those who brought them.'

(Tosefta *Sotah* 7.9)

In this light we may understand the duties given to Timothy at I Timothy 4.11 as those corresponding to the synagogue, and the functions of Timothy's church as synagogal. This situation would have come about because of the separation of the church and the synagogue, which meant that the church would have to adopt the functions of the synagogue as well as those which were peculiar to the church.

Because of the intellectual functions of the synagogue, a distinction arises between the presbyters, or elders, of the synagogue, at the head of whom might be an *archisynagogos* (synagogue leader), and the rabbinate. Thus the *archisynagogos* is effectively a patron, having no necessary qualification to teach. The following inscription dates from second century Jerusalem:

11) Theodotus, son of Vettenus and synagogue-ruler, son of a synagogue-ruler and grandson of a synagogue-ruler, built the synagogue for the reading of the law and instruction in the commandments; also the strangers' lodgings and the dining rooms and water facilities and hostel for the use of those from foreign lands. The foundation of this his fathers and the elders (*presbyteroi*) and Simonides laid.

(Inscription: CIJ 1404)

The dating of this inscription suggested here follows the recent suggestions of Kee.[4]

---

4   H C Kee, 'Defining the first century CE synagogue: problems and progress' in H C Kee and L Cohick (edd) *The Evolution of the synagogue* (TPI, Harrisburg, 1999), pp 7-26.

The inscription shows that the function of synagogue-ruler might be hereditary, and was dependent on wealth and the ability to offer patronage.[5] A similar pattern is shown by this, later, inscription:

12) The tomb of Joseph, synagogue-ruler, son of Joseph, a synagogue-ruler.

(Inscription: CIJ 584)

Although there is little evidence of an hereditary episcopate in early Christianity[6], it is certainly the case that office in early Christianity was dependent upon the same financial criteria. Thus, among others, Polycarp, Clement and Hermas were leaders of their Christian communities by virtue of their relatively high economic status and by virtue of their ability to offer patronage to the church. It is hard to chart developments within Judaism, as the later evidence is entirely rabbinic and inevitably presents the rabbinate as the only leadership within the synagogue. It is however possible that the intellectual leadership and the social leadership were for a time separate, just as, in Christian circles, the presbyters came to take on the teaching functions in their communities instead of the task of patronage.

Further reading:
James Tunstead Burtchaell, *From synagogue to church* (Cambridge University Press, 1992)
Lee I Levine (ed.), *The synagogue in late antiquity* (ASOR, Philadelphia Pa, 1987)

5   On the *Archisynagogos* as a patronal figure, see T Rajak and D Noy, 'Archisynagogos: office, title, and social status' in *JRS* 83 (1993), pp 75-93, at pp 87-89.
6   The only example of which the present writer is aware is the case of the Geminii, in third century Africa (Cyprian, *Letter* 1.)

3
Ordination

There is some evidence that Christian presbyters derived from the Jewish institution of elders.[7] The common use of the term would certainly indicate that this is the case. Less certain, however, is whether there is any parallel in the manner in which elders were appointed. I Timothy 4.14 indicates that the laying on of hands was part of ordination procedure in some parts of Christianity from the earliest period. Whether it is derived from Judaism is less certain. The following passage indicates that this might have been the case.

13) It is taught: 'The laying on of hands, and the laying on of hands of the elders is performed by three.' What do 'laying on of hands' and 'laying on of hands of the elders' mean?

R Yohanan said: '[The latter] refers to the ordination of elders.' Abaya said to Rab Joseph: 'Where do we learn that three are needed for the ordination of elders? From the scripture "And he (Moses) laid his hands upon him [Joshua]"?[8] If so, one is enough! And if you should object, Moses stood in place of seventy-one, then seventy-one should be the right number!' The difficulty remained unanswered.

R Aha the son of Raba asked R Ashi: 'Is ordination effected by the actual laying on of hands?' ['No'] he said, 'it is by the conferring of the degree. He is called by the name of Rabbi and given the authority to judge cases of *Kenas*.'

(BT *Sanhedrin* 13B)

However, this is simply part of a discussion of *semikah* (laying on hands) in BT *Sanhedrin*, discussing the teaching that the laying on of hands is by three, (the passage originally found in the Mishnah at this point, which did not relate to ordination at all!) Overall, it is possible to perceive a strategy here in the Talmud of denying that *semikah* is part of ordination. Given that the matter at hand is the 'ordination' of elders, it is possible that the issue has become controversial in the light of the Christian practice of laying hands upon presbyters (elders). The question is one of whether the ordination of elders by laying on hands actually derived from Christianity.

More evidence is available for ordination through seating.

14) And when he had finished [speaking these] words, Joshua again fell at the feet of Moses. And Moses grasped his hand and raised him into the seat before him . . .

(*Assumption of Moses* 12.1-2[9])

---

7   To which see the references at 15 below and 10 above.
8   The verse in question is Deut 34.9: 'And Moses laid his hands upon him.'
9   This is a work describing Moses' last instructions to Joshua, of very uncertain date. Suggestions range from the second century BCE to the second century CE.

This may illuminate the statement at Matthew 23.2 that the scribes and pharisees sit in the seat of Moses. Notice that there is no reference to a laying on of hands.

Appointment through seating was also known in the Sanhedrin.

15) And three rows of the disciples of the sages were seated before them, every one of whom knew his proper place. When it was necessary to appoint, one was appointed from the first row. One from the second row then came into the first, and one from the third came into the second. Then somebody from the assembly was chosen and was seated in the third row. But he did not sit in the place of the earlier one, but sat in the place which was assigned him.

(Mishnah *Sanhedrin* 4.4)

This may be the origin of the ordination of rabbis by seating. The word used for 'appoint' (*smk*) is the same as that used for ordination, as it was for the laying on of hands.

16) The members of the Nasi's household once appointed an incompetent teacher, and the Rabbis said to Judah bar Nahmani the translator of Resh Laqish: 'Go and stand beside him as an expounder.' Standing beside him, he bent down to listen to what he wished to teach, but the teacher did not commence to say anything.

(BT *Sanhedrin* 7B)

This indicates that the teacher is sitting, since Judah has to lean over to hear. Even Moses, at one point, has a 'seat of Moses'!

17) He (Moses) wrapped himself in his garment (*tallit*) and sat himself down like an elder (*zaqen*). Then the Holy One, blessed be He, said . . .

(*Exodus Rabbah* 43.4[10])

Similarly we may note:

18) Said R Simeon b Azzai, 'I have a tradition from the testimony of the seventy-two elders, on the day on which they seated R Eleazar b Azariah in the session, that the Song of Songs and Qoheleth impart uncleanness to hands.'

(*Song of Songs Rabbah* 1.20[11])

Early Christianity also knows the placing of a newly ordained person into a seat, and this may be a parallel and independent ordination rite known in Christianity alongside or separately from the laying on of hands. Thus see: *Canons of Hippolytus* 4; ps-Clement, *To James* 5 and *Homily* 3.60-72; Eusebius, *Ecclesiastical History* 6.29; and *Life of Polycarp* 22-23.

The rite of seating might have come about as a seated position was the normal position for teaching in the Graeco-Roman world. Thus:

---

10 This commentary on Exodus is of uncertain date, though it is assuredly relatively late.
11 This is a commentary on the Song of Songs dating from around the sixth century, though it contains much material of some antiquity.

19) On that day [the day on which R Gamaliel was deposed] many stools were added [in the *beit haMidrash*]. R. Yohanan said: 'There is a difference of opinion on this matter between Abba Joseph b. Dosethai and the Rabbis: one [authority] says that four hundred stools were added, and the other said seven hundred.'

(BT *Berakoth* 28A)

20) Said R. Judah: 'Any who have not seen the double colonnade [of the synagogue] of Alexandria in Egypt have not seen the glory of Israel in all their days. It was a kind of great basilica, one colonnade inside another. Sometimes there were twice as many people there as those who went forth from Egypt. There were seventy-one golden thrones set up there, corresponding to the seventy-one elders, each one worth twenty-five talents of gold, with a wooden platform in the middle. The leader of the synagogue stands on it, with flags in his hand. When one began to read, the other would wave the flags so they would answer, "Amen" upon each blessing. Then that one would wave the flags, and they would answer, "Amen".'

(Tosefta *Sukkah* 4.6)

The presbyters are seated in the apse of a basilica, in much the same way that Christian presbyters are described in *Passion of Perpetua* 12.

We may thus see the operation of the false prophet in Hermas *Mandate* 11, who is likewise seated on a chair, as pointing to a similar tendency to imitate the posture of the Graeco-Roman teacher within early Christianity.

Finally note:

21) When Rab was about to go to Babylon R Hiyyah said to Rabbi: 'My sister's son is going to Babylon. May he decide on matters of ritual law (*yihreh*)?' 'He may (*yihreh*).' 'May he decide cases (*yidin*)?' 'He may (*yidin*).'

(BT *Sanhedrin* 5A-B)

There is the possibility that here there is a formula of announcement of ordination.

Further reading

Arnold Ehrhardt, 'Jewish and Christian ordination' in *JEH* 5 (1954), pp 125-138

Lawrence A Hoffmann, 'Jewish ordination on the eve of Christianity' in W Vos and G Wainwright (edd.) *Ordination rites: papers read at the 1979 congress of Societas Liturgica* (Liturgical Ecumenical Center Trust, Rotterdam, 1980), pp 11-41

Edward J Kilmartin, 'Ministry and ordination in early Christianity' in W Vos and G Wainwright (edd.) *Ordination rites: papers read at the 1979 congress of Societas Liturgica* (Liturgical Ecumenical Center Trust, Rotterdam, 1980), pp 42-69

4
Corporate prayer

Firstly it is to be noted that prayer in early Judaism was not generally corporate, but individual.

> **22)** R. Gamaliel says, 'Every day a person should pray the Eighteen [Benedictions].'
>
> R. Joshua says, 'The content of the Eighteen.'
>
> R. Aqiba says, 'If his prayer is fluent he prays the Eighteen [Benedictions.] But if not, the content of the Eighteen.'
>
> R Eliezer says: 'He that makes his prayer a fixed task, his prayer is no supplication.'
>
> (Mishnah *Berakoth* 4.3-4)

Corporate prayer demands fixed forms, whereas here a degree of fluidity is envisaged. The eighteen benedictions to which reference is made are those which are said to have been arranged by Simeon ha-Pakuli at Yabneh.[12] Known otherwise as the *tefillah*, or as the *'amidah*, the nucleus of these eighteen prayers (fewer on festival days) certainly precedes Yabneh and may originate in Jerusalem[13], though it is probable that some ordering of the *tefillah* took place at Yabneh.[14] At this point there may have been some movement towards corporate prayer.

> **23)** Said R. Meir, 'Once we were sitting in the house of study before R. Aqiba, and we were reciting the shema' and we could not hear ourselves because of a certain inquisitor who was standing before the doorway.' They said to him, '[A precedent from] a time of danger is not proof [that such a practice is proper].'
>
> (Tosefta *Berakoth* 2.13)

Here there seems some movement towards fixed formulae, though the date of this tale is uncertain. Notably this is taking place in a house of study rather than in a service of corporate worship. There were of course exceptions, and the whole matter was clearly debated.

> **24)** R. Judah would respond together with the prayer leader, 'Holy, holy, holy ... [is the Lord of Hosts; the whole earth is full of his glory' (Is. 6.3)], and 'Blessed ... [be the glory of the Lord in its place' (Ezek. 3.12).] All these R. Judah would recite together with the prayer-leader.
>
> (Tosefta *Berakoth* 1.9)

---

12 BT *Berakoth* 28B-29A, quoted at passage 1 above.
13 So E L Bickerman, 'The Civic Prayer for Jerusalem' in *HThR* 55(1962), pp 163-85
14 See in particular the suggestions of Tzvee Zahavy, 'The politics of piety' in Bradshaw and Hoffmann, *Making*, pp 42-68.

The formula 'Holy, holy, holy *etc.*' appears in one of the blessings which accompany the *shema*ʿ; that R Judah is joining in indicates that the prayer is being said publicly.

One may not deduce from such passages as that following, from Josephus, who is quoting a gentile enactment, that corporate prayer was known in an earlier period, as the citizens of Sardis might not have understood the nature of Jewish religion and as there is no indication that the prayer is actually corporate:

25) Agreed by the council and the people, on a motion introduced by the magistrates: Whereas the Jewish citizens who dwell in our city have received many and significant favours from the people, and have now come before the council and the people appealing that, since their laws and their freedom have been restored by the Roman senate and people, they might gather and conduct their affairs and adjudicate lawsuits following their accepted customs, and that a place should be given them where they might gather, together with the women and children, to offer their ancestral prayers and sacrifices to God . . .

(Josephus *Jewish Antiquities* 14.260)

The nature of this debate may explain why early Christians do not appear corporately to have recited the Lord's Prayer; that is to say, it was understood as an individual prayer. Certainly its closest parallel occurs in individual prayer:

26) If somebody prays concerning what has already happened, his prayer is pointless. Thus, if somebody whose wife is pregnant says: 'May it be pleasing to God that my wife bear a male', that prayer is pointless.

(Mishnah *Berakoth* 9.3)

A further matter for debate was the content of the prayer, and in particular the relative significance of what came to be the two main elements in the synagogue service, the *shema*ʿ ('Hear, O Israel . . . ') which was said with accompanying benedictions, and the *tefillah*.

27) Those who write [Torah] scrolls, phylacteries, and *mezzuzot* pause [their work] to recite the *Shema*ʿ, but do not pause for the ʿ*Amidah* [the eighteen benedictions]. Rab says: 'Just as they do not pause for the ʿ*Amidah*, so they do not pause for the recitation of the *shema*ʿ.' R. Haninah b. Aqiba says: 'Just as they pause for the recitation of the *shema*ʿ, so they pause for the *Amidah*.' Said R. Eleazar bar Zadok: 'When Rab Gamaliel and his court were in Yabneh and they were busy with community necessities, they did not pause [their work] so as not to disturb their concentration.'

(Tosefta *Berakoth* 2.6)

There is no doubt that both the *shema*ʿ, with accompanying benedictions, and the *tefillah*, were known in Judaism at the time of the formation of Christianity. However, the extent to which either might be said to be normative within Judaism is debatable. Thus note:

28) [And when the sun a]ri[ses to illuminate the earth they shall bless. And when they begin to speak they shall say: Blessed be the God of Israel] who declare[s . . .] for tod[ay . . .] festivals of glor[y . . .] he shall fulfil his glor[y . . . Peace be upon you] Israel. [. . .] And on the sixth of the mo[nth, in the evening they shall bless. And when they begin to speak they shall say: Blessed be the God of Israel . . .] night which h[e? . . .] we, together with the holy one[s . . .] to fiv[e . . . and [. . .] and when [the sun arises . . .] ? . . . [. . .] light of day that we may know [. . .] in the six gates of ligh[t . . . And we] the sons of your covenant shall praise [your name . . .] together with all the companies [of light . . . a]ll the tongues of knowledge. Bless[. . . ?lig]ht. The seventh of the [month, in the evening they shall bless. When they begin to speak] they [shall say:] Blessed be the God of Is[rael . . .] righteousness . . . [. . .] [al]l these things we know through [. . .] Blessed be the G[od of Israel . . .]
[And when] the sun [arises] to illuminate the ear[th, they shall bless . . .]
[. . .] together with the companies of light. Today [. . .] the ninth day . . .
[The twel]fth of the month, in the evening [they shall bless . . .] [. . .] And we, his holy people, rejoice this night [. . .] us the witnesses of the service of the day [. . .]
God of lights . . . [. . .] the light and the witness[es . . .] . . . the lig[ht of day] [Blessed be] your [na]me, God of Israel, in a[ll . . .] [. . .] [holy of ho]lies in the heights . . . his holy na[me . . .] and glory in the ho[ly of holies . . .] and witnesses for us in the holy of holies [. . .] [. . .] in the dominion of the light of the day. Blessed [. . .] [. . . p]eace be with you I[srael . . .] [. . . bles]sed be the God of Israel, who performs won[ders . . .] [. . .] the earth. And the night . . . [. . .] who for us adds [. . .] all its divisions for him. [. . .] God of Israe[l] [. . .] your holiness [. . .] on the thir[tieth . . .] twelve[. . .] [. . . I]srael [. . .] your [holi]ness . . .
And when [the sun] arises [. . .] the vault of the hea[v]ens they shall bless. And when they begin to speak [they shall say: Blessed be the Go[d of Israel . . .] To[d]ay he renewed[. . .] in the fourt[eenth of the gates of light . . .] for us the rule [. . .] [. . . ?four]teen compa[nies of . . .] the heat of the [sun . . .] when it crosses [. . . with the migh[t of his powerful hand] [. . . Peace be upon you, Israel.] In the fif[teenth of the month, in the ev]ening, they shall bless. When they begin to speak they shall say: Blessed be the G[od of Israel] who hides [. . .] before his countenance in every division of his glory. And that night [. . .] . . . et]ernal and to give him thanks. [And] our deliverance at the beginn[ing of . . .] [. . .] the rotations of the great lights. [And] today, fourte[en [. . .] the light of the day. P[eace be upon] you Israel. [. . .] [And when the sun arises] to illuminate the earth, they shall bless. Wh[en they begin to speak they shall say:] [Blessed be the God of Israel . . . wh]ich are for the festivals of joy and the celebrations of glo[ry . . .] [. . . in the fi[fteenth of the gate[s of light . . .] in the divisions of the night . . .

(4Q 503, fragments 4, 7-11, 13-16, 1-3)

This is indicative of corporate prayer in the morning and the evening entirely separate from the *shema⁽* and *tefillah*. Nonetheless, and in spite of the fragmentary condition of this scroll, in the thanksgiving for the light, as in the extent to which praise is said to be given together with the heavenly hosts, we may catch a glimpse of the *yotzer*, with its accompanying *qedusha*, which is one of the thanksgivings which accompany the *shema⁽*.[15] It is perhaps stretching the evidence somewhat to see hints in the evening prayers here of the thanksgiving for the day past which appears in *Apostolic Tradition* 25, though in favour of this it is to be noted that the same chapter has a meal practice which seems rooted in Jewish custom.

Apart from the extent to which the *shema⁽* and the *tefillah* might be said to have been normative within early Judaism, the extent to which they were adopted within Christianity, is more debatable. Thus although *Apostolic Constitutions* 7 contains a barely Christianized version of the *tefillah*, this is as likely to have derived directly from Judaism in the conditions of the fourth century in Syria as to have been a survival from earliest times.[16] A more likely candidate to be a Christian prayer historically rooted in the *tefillah* is the liturgical fragment to be found among the Egerton Papyri, which Marmorstein thinks is a form of the *tefillah*.[17]

One part of the complex of Jewish prayer surrounding the *shema⁽* which certainly found its way into Christian practice is the recitation of the Decalogue.

29) The leader said to them, 'Bless with one blessing.'
They blessed, pronounced the Ten Commandments, the *shema⁽*, *And it shall come to pass if you shall hearken* (Deut. 11.13-21), and *And the Lord spoke to Moses* (Numbers 15.37-41), and they blessed the people with three blessings: True and sure, the *abodah*, and the priestly blessing.

(Mishnah *Tamid* 5.1)

Note that only one blessing is pronounced before the *shema⁽*, rather than the two which became more widespread in later periods.[18] This is an indication that some credibility is to be attached to this account, even though it is not to be swallowed whole as situated in the Temple. Support for the recitation of the Decalogue at this time may then be got from:

30) He Moses also commands that 'on going to bed and rising' people should meditate on the ordinances of God.

(*Letter of Aristeas* 160[19])

15 A suggestion cautiously made by M Smith, 'On the *yotser* and related texts' in Levine, *Synagogue in late antiquity.*
16 See the discussion by David A Fiensy *Prayers alleged to be Jewish* (Scholars Press, Chico Ca, 1985).
17 A Marmorstein 'The Oldest Form of the Eighteen Benedictions' in *JQR* 34 (1943-44), pp 137-59. The fragment is found at H I Bell and T C Skeat, *Fragments of an unknown Gospel* (British Museum, London, 1935), pp 58-59.
18 P Sigal, 'Early Christian and rabbinic liturgical affinities' in *NTS* 30 (1984), pp 63-90 at p 72, suggests the second of the two, which concerns God's unchanging love for Israel shown through the Torah and stresses the divine unity was formed in response to Christianity.
19 Although the precise date of this letter, purporting to tell of the manner in which the Jewish law was translated into Greek at Alexandria, a date before the parting of the ways is fairly assured.

This is in addition to support from the Nash papyrus, which gives the Decalogue followed by the shema[.20] The Babylonian Talmud however reckons that the practice of reciting the decalogue was abandoned because of heretics.

31) 'They recited the Ten Words, the *shema[*, the sections "And it shall happen if you diligently hearken", and "And He said", "True and firm", the *Abodah*, and the priestly benediction.'

Rab Judah said in the name of Samuel: 'Outside the precincts [of Jerusalem], people sought to recite the same, but they were prohibited on account of the rebellion of the *minim.*' Similarly it has been taught: R. Nathan says, 'They sought to do the same outside the Temple, but it had long been abolished on account of the rebellion of the *minim.*' Rabbah b. Bar Hanah hoped to establish this in Sura, but R. Hisda said to him, it had long been abolished on account of the rebellion of the *minim.* Amemar hoped to establish it in Nehardea, but R. Ashi said to him, it had long been abolished on account of the rebellion of the *minim.*

(BT *Berakoth* 12A)

These *minim* could be Christians. Pliny's account of Christianity in Bithynia that Christians maintained that 'they bound themselves with an oath, not for any crime, but not to commit theft or robbery or adultery, not to break their word, and not to deny a deposit when demanded'[21] could thus be a reference to the Decalogue.[22]

As we have noted, benedictions accompanied the *shema[*. Hammer points out that it is not necessarily the case that Mishnah *Tamid* 5.1 refers to one of those which today precedes the Torah, but may be a more general ascription of praise to God.[23] Nonetheless, as we noted above, there are hints of the benediction called the *yotzer*, which is a thanksgiving for light and which includes the *qedusha* ('Holy, holy, holy . . . ') in the prayers from Qumran. There are thus grounds to support the suggestion that the eucharistic prayer of Addai and Mari is modelled on the benedictions which surround the *shema[*.[24]

At the end of all this, perhaps the most that can be said is that there was a widespread and well-established pattern of prayer in early Judaism in the morning and evening, though elsewhere prayer at the ninth hour is additionally known, and that the *shema[* and the decalogue were frequently part of that prayer.

32) Before the rising of the sun they [the Essenes] do not speak of mundane matters, but offer to him certain ancestral prayers, as though begging him to rise.

(Josephus *Jewish War* 2.128-129)

20   For a discussion of this papyrus see F C. Burkitt, 'The Hebrew papyrus of the ten commandments' in *JQR* 15 (1903), pp 392-408.
21   Pliny, *Letter* 10.96.
22   See on this G Vermes, 'The decalogue and the minim' in *Post-biblical Jewish studies* (Brill, Leiden, 1975).
23   R Hammer, 'What did they bless: a study of Mishnah Tamid 5.1' in *JQR* 81 (1990-1991) pp 305-324.
24   So J Vellian, 'The anaphoral structure of Addai and Mari' in *Le Muséon* 85 (1972), pp 201-223.

33) [Moses instructed] 'Twice each day, at the dawn thereof and when the hour comes for turning to repose, let all acknowledge before God the bounties which he has bestowed on them through their deliverance from the land of Egypt.' Thanksgiving is a natural duty, and is rendered alike in gratitude for past mercies and to incline the giver to others yet to come.

(Josephus *Jewish Antiquities* 4.212)

34) As day and night come on, I shall enter the covenant of God, and when evening and morning pass on, I shall repeat his precepts.

(1QS 10.10)

35) On three occasions in the year priests raise up their hands [in the priestly benediction] four times a day, at the dawn prayer, the additional prayer, the afternoon prayer, and the closing of the gates. On occasion of fasts, on the occasions of [prayers of members of the] delegation [*maamad*], and on the Day of Atonement.

(Mishnah *Taanith* 4.1)

This is an attempt to align the practice of daily prayer with that found in villages which prayed at the same time as the sacrifices of the Temple. The strategy does not succeed because there is no actual alignment. The threefold practice does however explain the insistence of the *Didache* that prayer be offered three times daily. Additionally the fasting practice enjoined by the *Didache*, which is adopted in contradistinction to that of the 'hypocrites' can be explained through current Jewish practice.

36) The following ten enactments were ordained by Ezra: That the law be read in the *Minhah* service on Sabbath; that the law be read on the second and fifth [days; i.e., Mondays and Thursdays]; that courts be held on the second and fifth . . .

(BT *Baba Qamma* 82A)

Further reading

P F Bradshaw, *Daily Prayer in the Early Church* (SPCK, London, 1981)

P F Bradshaw and L A Hoffmann (edd.), *The making of Jewish and Christian Worship* (University of Notre Dame, Notre Dame, 1981)

S Reif, 'Some liturgical issues in the talmudic sources' in *Studia Liturgica* 16 (1982-83), pp 188-206

5
Immersions and purifications

Early Judaism knew a variety of washings and purifications. It is not the task of the editors to determine which, if any, were the basis for the Christian practice of baptism, but to present some of the available evidence.

37) One should not go through the waters to approach the pure food of the men of sanctity, for one is not cleansed unless one turns away from wickedness . . .

(1QS 5.14)

38) Nobody shall enter the courtyard for the service, even if he is clean, until he immerses.
On this day the high priest must immerse five times and perform sanctification [of the hands and feet] ten times, on all occasions, with this exception, in the *Parwah* chamber in the temple.

(Mishnah *Yoma* 3.3)

39) Until the fifth hour they [the Essenes] work strenuously, when once more they assemble in one place and, girding themselves with linen cloths, they bathe their bodies in cold waters. After this purification they assemble in a private apartment which none of the uninitiated is allowed to enter and, as they are now themselves pure, they repair to the refectory, as though going to some sacred shrine.

(Josephus *Jewish War* 2.129-131)

40) They [the Essenes] are divided according to the duration of their discipline into four grades; the junior members are so much inferior to the seniors, that if a senior is only touched by a junior, he must bathe as though he had suffered contact with an outsider.

(Josephus *Jewish War* 2.150)

41) A man who has had a nocturnal emission and who does not have water in which to immerse himself, 'Behold, he may recite the *shema*' silently.' . . . the words of R. Meir.

(Tosefta *Berakoth* 2.13)

42) One who is in mourning may, after he has immersed, eat the Passover offering in the evening, but he may not eat of hallowed things.

(Mishnah *Pesahim* 8.8)

43) He decreed immersion for men to whom pollution had happened. This was an enactment founded on the biblical text; as it is written: 'If a man has an emission of semen, he shall bathe his whole body in water. .' [Lev 15.16] This was an enactment founded on the biblical text: in reference to *terumah* and sacrifices. He came and decreed that even for [the study of the] words of Torah [immersion is needed].

(BT *Baba Qamma* 82B)

44) R Judah said in the name of Rab: 'Thus was the habit of R Judah ben Elai: on Friday someone brought him a basin of warm water. Then he washed his face, his hands and his feet, and wrapped himself and sat in fringed robes, and was like an angel of the Lord of Hosts.'

(BT *Shabbath* 25B)

More positively the following direct link with Christian practice may be observed:

45) . . . More excellent are smitten waters which render clean such time as they are flowing water. More excellent than they are living waters, for they serve for the immersion of them that have a flux, and for the sprinkling of lepers and are valid for mixing with the ashes of the sin offering.

(Mishnah *Mikwaoth* 1.8)

Further definition of what is intended here is given elsewhere:

46) R Zadok bore witness that if running water were more than the dripping water it was valid.

(Mishnah *Eduyoth* 7.3)

This conforms entirely with the preferred practice of the *Didache*. Even though the justification may differ, this is likely in any event to be secondary, and the practice of the *Didache* as regards baptism has derived from Jewish practice and Jewish preference for flowing water.

A further Christian prescription may be illuminated from the same tractate of the Mishnah:

47) If a menstruant put coins in her mouth and went down and immersed herself, she is clean of her impurity, but made unclean again by her saliva. If she put her hair in her mouth or closed her hand or pressed her lips together it is as though she had not immersed herself at all.

(Mishnah *Mikwaoth* 8.5)

This illuminates the prescription of *Apostolic Tradition* 21 that women being baptized should remove all jewellery and loosen their hair. Further witness is borne to this practice elsewhere in the Talmud, in a discussion of the enactment of Ezra that a woman should comb her hair before immersion.

48) This was an enactment founded on the biblical text; as it is taught: 'And he shall wash his flesh in water . . . [Lev 14:9]' that there should not be anything externally between his flesh and the water; his flesh [includes] and that which is attached to his flesh, that is, the hair. One may say that as far as the biblical enactment goes it would only have to be necessary to see that the hair should not be knotted or there should not be anything which might intervene, whereas Ezra came and decreed actual combing.

(BT *Baba Qamma* 82A-B)

A special class of washings in Judaism was the baptism of proselytes, concerning which the Talmud gives the following instructions:

49) Our Rabbis taught: 'If at this time a man wants to become a proselyte, he must be asked: "What reason do have you for wanting to become a proselyte; do you not know that Israel at this time is afflicted and oppressed, despised, harassed and overcome by afflictions?" If he says, "I know and I am not worthy", he should be received immediately, and he should be taught in some of the lesser and some of the greater commandments. He should be taught about the sin [of the neglect of the commandments] about gleanings, about the forgotten sheaf, the corner, and the tithe of the poor. He should be taught of the punishment for the transgression of the commandments. Furthermore, thus : "Be it known to you that before you came to this condition, if you had eaten suet you would not have been punished with *kareth*, if you had desecrated the Sabbath you would not have been punished with stoning; but now were you to eat suet you would be punished with *kareth*; were you to desecrate the Sabbath you would be punished with stoning." And just as he is told of the punishment for the transgression of the commandments, so is he informed of the reward granted for their fulfillment. He should be told, "Know that the world to come was made only for the righteous, and all of Israel at this time is unable to accept either too much abundance, or too much retribution."

He should not, however, be persuaded or dissuaded too much. If he accepted, he is circumcised right away. If there remain on him any shreds which invalidates the circumcision, he should be circumcised a second time. When he is healed, arrangements are made for his immediate immersion; two learned men should stand by his side and make known to him some of the lesser commandments and some of the greater ones. When he comes up after his immersion, he is considered as an Israelite in all matters.

In the case of a woman [proselyte], women should make her sit in the water up to her neck, while two learned men should stand by her outside and should make known to her some of the lesser commandments and some of the greater ones.

As for a proselyte so for an emancipated slave; and in the place where a menstruant performs her immersion, there may a proselyte and an emancipated slave perform the immersion; and whatever is deemed an interception in [ritual] immersion is also deemed to be an interception in the immersions of a proselyte, an emancipated slave and a menstruant.

(BT *Yebamoth* 47A-B)

The date at which such a practice was instituted is, however, highly uncertain. Were it demonstrably in widespread existence before the parting of the ways then it would provide an obvious origin for Christian baptism. However such evidence is lacking, although it has been suggested that the following passage is indicative of the existence of proselyte baptism in the second century BCE.[25] However it is equally probable that the purifications to which reference is made are those which women would normally undergo. They are unlawful because the women are gentiles.

> 50) You shall take as wives the daughters of the gentiles, purifying them with an unlawful purification . . .
>
> (*Testament of Levi* 14.6)

Although the date of the institution of proselyte baptism is uncertain, the directions that such baptism take place according to the regulations surrounding the purification of women after menstruation once again fit in with the directions given in Hippolytus' *Apostolic Tradition* 21. Further indication that proselyte baptism originated in the nexus of purifications surrounding levitical purity is provided by the following:

> 51) If a man become a proselyte on the day before Passover, the school of Shammai say he may immerse himself and consume his Passover offering in the evening. And the school of Hillel say that he that separates himself from his uncircumcision is like one that separates himself from a grave.
>
> (Mishnah *Eduyoth* 5.2)

In other words a single immersion is insufficient, but further sprinklings are necessary. The discussion implies moreover that the status of a baptized proselyte was still unclear in the second century. The implication is thus that Christian baptism and proselyte baptism both derived from the ritual purification incumbent upon any who was unclean (a gentile being unclean by nature) but that they were independent growths from the same shoot. Further evidence for this is provided by the following discussion:

> 52) If a proselyte has been circumcised but has not yet bathed [he is a proselyte.] Everything depends on the circumcision. This is according to Rab Eliezer, but Rab Aqiba said: 'Also [the lack of] bathing is a bar.'
>
> (BT *Gerim* 60A)

A much longer discussion of this issue is found at BT *Yebamoth* 46A-46B.

Becoming a Jew was not the only context in which promises and vows might be tied up to the initiation process. Within Judaism, washing, preceded by

---

25 By Louis Finkelstein, 'The institution of baptism for proselytes' in *JBL* 52 (1933), pp 203-211. *The Testament of Levi* (from which citation 54 is also taken) is one of a series of death-bed testaments pseudonymously ascribed to the twelve sons of Jacob, dating from the second century BCE.

instruction and accompanied by promises, might signify entry into different groups.

53) Before he [an Essene initiate] may touch the common food he is made to swear tremendous oaths.

(Josephus Jewish War 2.139)

Many early Christian baptismal rituals involved anointing. According to Munier, the following passage provides evidence of the Jewish starting-point of such rituals.[26]

54) I saw seven men in white clothing, who were saying to me: 'Arise, put on the vestments of the priesthood, the crown of righteousness, the oracle of understanding, the robe of truth, the breastplate of faith, the mitre for the head, and the apron for prophetic power.' Each carried one of these and put them on me and said: 'from now on be a priest, you and all your posterity.' The first anointed me with holy oil and gave me a staff. The second washed me with pure water, fed me by hand with bread and holy wine, and put on me a holy and glorious vestment. The third put on me something made of linen like an ephod.

(Testament of Levi 8.2-5)

Whereas the parallels are obvious, the context is that of a vision in which Levi learns of the future of his tribe as kings and priests. If this is a reference to baptismal anointing it is unique, as the typology of kingship and priesthood is not generally attached to pre-baptismal anointing. Furthermore this hypothesis does nothing to explain post-baptismal anointing.

Further reading:
Adele Yarbro Collins, 'The origin of Christian Baptism' in M E Johnson (ed.), *Living Water, Sealing Spirit* (Liturgical Press, Collegeville, 1995), pp 35-57
J Delorme, 'The practice of baptism in Judaism at the beginning of the Christian era' in *Baptism in the New Testament: a symposium* (Geoffrey Chapman, London, 1964) pp 25-60

---

26 Charles Munier, 'Initiation chrétienne et rites d'onction (IIe-IIIe siècles)' in *Revue des sciences religieuses* 64 (1990), pp 115-125.

6
Reading and preaching

We have already noted the extent to which the reading of the Scriptures was fundamental to the worship of the synagogue. The following is a short section of a debate in the Babylonian Talmud interpreting Mishnah *Megillah* 3.4: 'On the new moon of Adar which coincided with the Sabbath—they read the pericope of *Sheqels* [Ex. 30.11-16]'

> **55)** ... An objection was raised: 'When the new moon of Adar falls on Sabbath, the portion of *Sheqalim* is read, and *Jehoiada the Priest* is read as *haftarah*'. Now according to the one who says that *When you take* should be read, there is a good reason for reading *Jehoiada the Priest* as *haftarah*, because it is similar to it, as it is written [there], *the money from the assessment of persons*. But according to the one who says that *My food which is offered to me* is read, is it similar? It is, on the basis of R. Tabi's dictum [which was mentioned earlier in the chapter].
>
> The following was then cited in objection: 'If it [the New Moon of Adar] falls on the portion next to it [the portion of *Sheqalim*], either before or after, they read it and repeat it'. Now this creates no difficulty for one who holds that *When you take* is read because [the regular portion containing this passage] falls at that time. But according to the one who says that *My food which is offered to me* is read, does [the portion containing that passage] fall at that time?' 'Yes, for those to the west of Damascus [i.e., Palestine], who complete the reading of the Pentateuch in three years.'
>
> (BT *Megillah* 29B)

The point of citing this debate is to note that, whereas by this stage (the fifth century CE) a three-year cycle is established in Palestine, in Babylon there is still much dispute, in particular with fitting the festal calendar in with a system of *lectio continua* and with regard to the *haftarah*. This implies that lectionary systems are still developing, and that theories concerning early Christianity which depend on retrojecting a three-year lectionary cycle into first-century Palestine[27] are without foundation.

It is however possible to understand some early Christian documents in the light of the preaching and reading practice of the synagogue. It must be recognized that the Hebrew would not be 'understanded of the common people' and a translation was always given. The procedure is regulated thus.

> **56)** He that reads in the law may not read less than three verses; he may not read more than one verse to the interpreter, or, in the prophets, three verses; but if these three are three separate paragraphs he reads them out one by one. They may skip verses in the prophets, but one may not skip in the law. How much may he skip? Only so much that he does not oblige the interpreter to make a pause.
>
> (Mishnah *Megillah* 4.4)

---

27 Such as that of M Goulder, *Midrash and Lection in Matthew* (SPCK, London, 1974).

The antiquity of this provision may be illustrated from an ancient Jewish homily from around the first century BCE, which clearly skips verses in this manner.

57) Like judges the seafarers asked: 'Where are you from and what is your people, and what is your business?' [Jonah 1.8] When they had sought this out and discovered it, they did not fail to act justly, quite the opposite, for they had read that whoever is judged should himself sit in judgement. They said 'What shall we do with you? [Jonah1.11] You judge and decide!'

(Ps-Philo *On Jonah*)

It is widely accepted that this procedure, known as the targum, was the origin of preaching in the synagogue, as verses and phrases might be expanded in the process of translation. This procedure might lead to narrative homilies such as that on Jonah just cited, and likewise another on the same subject:

58) As he was running back and forth beside the sea in his agitation, he saw there a trireme. He waved to the seamen, and called out 'Where are you heading sailors? Where are you taking your ship? Do me a favour and bring me on board.' They said where they were going, reached an agreement and pulled him on board the ship. As they did so, the uproar of the sea became dangerous for the sailors. For as the prophet, the messenger to the town, boarded the ship, he found himself, because of his prophecy, in the waves of agitation. They took a stone onto the ship, in the shape of him who had taken on proclamation, and were sailing against themselves. Instead of sailing over the waves, the waves were rolling over them.

(Ps-Philo *On Jonah*)

The influence of this narrative homily might be seen in Christianity in the elaborate narrative of the slaughter of the firstborn in Melito of Sardis *On Pascha*, or in Hippolytus' description of the entry of the ark into Jerusalem in his homily *On the Psalms*.

Secondly, a passage might be broken down into its components for comment. Such a procedure is found in the early Tannaitic period being employed by R Eliezer b Hyrcanus:

59) . . . His father went up to disinherit him [R Eliezer ben Hyrcanos], and found him sitting and interpreting. The great ones of the region were sitting before him: Ben Zizzith Hakkesth, Naqdimon ben Gurion, and Ben Kalgba Shabua. He found him sitting and interpreting this verse: 'The wicked draw their swords and bend their bows . . .' (Ps 37.14) This refers to Amraphel and his companions. '. . . to cast down the poor and needy.' This refers to Lot. '. . . to slay those upright in their ways.' This refers to Abraham. 'Their sword enters their own heart . . .' (Ps 37.15) 'And he divided [his troops] against them at night, he and his retainers, and he struck them down.' (Gen 14.15)

(*Genesis Rabbah* 42[28])

---

28   Genesis Rabbah is an exegetical commentary on Genesis from the fifth century.

Such a procedure, according to Borgen, underlies the homiletic construction of John 6.36-58, which is based on the text 'he gave them bread from heaven to eat.'[29] I have suggested elsewhere that it may likewise be found in the seventh Mandate of Hermas.[30]

Similarly parables might be the basis for a homiletic address.

60) As R Yohanan said: ' When R Meir used to deliver his public discourses, a third was halakah, a third haggadah and a third consisted of parables.'

(BT *Sanhedrin* 38B)

This procedure can be found within early Christianity in the Similitudes of Hermas (which as I have pointed out in another context are otherwise very close to Jewish parables of the period)[31] and plausibly in the parable of the slave and the Son in John 8.31-58.[32]

A form of exhortation, particularly prominent in Hebrews, though also found in other early Christian documents such as *2 Clement*, is that which Wills has termed the 'word of exhortation.'[33] An example is held up to the audience for imitation, and exhortation is built onto that example. Wills is unable to find an example in rabbinic Judaism, but the following may be noted:

61) They used to bring out the ark into the open space in the town and put wood ashes on the ark and on the heads of the president and the father of the court; and every one took (of the ashes) and put them on his head. The eldest among them uttered before them words of admonition: 'Brothers, it is not written of the men of Nineveh that God saw their sack-cloth and their fasting, but "and God saw their works, that they turned from their evil way"; and in his protest (the prophet) says "rend your heart and not your garments."'

(Mishnah *Taanith* 2.1)

The close relationship between the assembly and the school has already been observed. This extended to preaching. Thus the following tale is told also in *Esther Rabbah* 1.1, where the audience is in a schoolroom.

62) R. Aqiba was sitting and interpreting and the congregation became drowsy. Wanting to rouse them, he said, 'What worthiness was in Esther that she ruled over one hundred twenty-seven provinces? Only that Esther was the descendant of Sarah, who lived one hundred twenty-seven years, so that she (Esther) ruled over one hundred twenty-seven provinces.'

(*Genesis Rabbah* 58.3)

---

29   Peder Borgen, *Bread from Heaven: an exegetical study of the concept of manna in the Gospel of John and the writings of Philo* (Brill, Leiden, 1965).
30   A Stewart-Sykes, 'Hermas and Hippolytus: Two Roman Preachers and their Audiences' in Mary B Cunningham and Pauline Allen (edd), *Preacher and Audience: Studies in Greek and Byzantine homiletics* (Brill, Leiden, 1998), pp 33-63, at pp 40-41.
31   A Stewart-Sykes, 'The Christology of Hermas and the interpretation of the fifth Similitude' in *Augustinianum* 37 (1997), at p 280.
32   Such is the argument of Barnabas Lindars, *Behind the Fourth Gospel* (SPCK, London, 1971), pp 44-47.
33   Lawrence Wills, 'The form of the sermon in Hellenistic Judaism and early Christianity' in *HThR* 77 (1984), pp 277-299.

Finally, it should be noted that the earliest form of preaching in Christianity was prophetic, and that scriptural preaching came about in the second or third generation, and is first witnessed in the Pastoral Epistles. This may be termed 'synagogalization.' One rabbi at least was conscious that a similar state of affairs had come about within Judaism!

63) Rabbi Abdimi from Haifa said: 'Since the day the Temple was destroyed, prophecy has been taken from the prophets and given to the sages [wise] . . .'

(BT *Baba Bathra* 12A)

Further reading:
Alistair Stewart-Sykes, *From prophecy to preaching* (Brill, Leiden, 2001)

7
Pascha and Passover

The following poem is found in targum *Neofiti* to Exodus, a translation into Aramaic of Exodus, dating probably from the first century BCE.

64) This is the night kept and fixed for deliverance in the name of YHWH when the children of Israel went out freed from the land of Egypt. Indeed, four nights have been written in the book of memorials.

The first night was when YHWH revealed himself to the world in order to create it. The world was waste and void and darkness was spread over the surface of the abyss, and the word of YHWH was the light and gave light. It was called the first night.

The second night was when YHWH revealed himself to Abraham aged 100 years and Sara his wife aged 90 years, so that what Scripture said might be fulfilled. And Isaac was 37 years when he was offered on the altar. The heavens came down and abased themselves and Isaac saw their perfections, and his eyes were darkened because of their perfections. It was called the second night.

The third night was when YHWH revealed himself against the Egyptians in the middle of the night. His hand slew the firstborn of the Egyptians and his right hand protected the firstborn of Israel in order to fulfill what Scripture said: my first born son is Israel. It was called the third night.

The fourth night will be when the world fulfils its end in order to be dissolved. The yokes of iron will be broken and the generations of impiety annihilated. And Moses will come out from the desert, and the King Messiah will emerge from on high. This is the night of Passover for the name of YHWH: a night kept and fixed for the salvation of all the generations of Israel.

(From Targum *Neofiti Exodus* 12.42)

These same paschal themes, creation, the binding of Isaac, the slaughter of the firstborn and the eschatological hope all appear prominently in the paschal liturgies of early Christianity, most particularly in Melito of Sardis's *On Pascha*. Our possession of *On Pascha* enables us to state with more confidence than with any other rite that in the paschal celebrations of those Christians who kept a festival at the time of the *Pesah*, subsequently known as Quartodecimans, there is a Christian practice which is clearly rooted in Jewish practice. Jewish practice must, however, be reconstructed, as ever, from later sources, and in particular the Mishnah tractate on *Pesah*. The following directions for the keeping of a domestic celebration are given there.

65) On the eve of Passover, from about the time of the evening offering, a man must eat nothing until nightfall. Even the poorest person in Israel must not eat unless he sits down to table, and they must not give them less than four cups of wine to drink, even if it is from the [paupers'] dish. After they have mixed him his first cup, the school of Shammai say: 'He says the benediction first over the day and then the benediction over the wine.' And the school of Hillel say: 'He says the benediction first over the wine and then the benediction over the day.'

When food is brought before him he eats it seasoned with lettuce, until he is come to the breaking of bread; they bring before him unleavened bread and lettuce and the *haroseth*, although *haroseth* is not a religious obligation. R Eliezer b R Zadok says: 'It is a religious obligation.' And in the holy city they used to bring before him the body of the Passover-offering.

They then mix him the second cup. And here the son asks his father (and if the son has not enough understanding his father instructs him) 'Why is this night different from other nights? For on other nights we eat seasoned food once, but this night twice; on other nights we eat leavened or unleavened bread, but this night all is unleavened; on other nights we eat flesh roast, stewed, or cooked, but this night all is roast; on other nights we dip but once, but this night twice.' And according to the understanding of the son his father instructs him. He begins with the disgrace and ends with the glory; and he expounds from 'A wandering Aramaean was my father . . .' until he finishes the whole section.

Rabban Gamaliel used to say: 'Whosoever has not said these three things at Passover has not fulfilled his obligation. And these are they: Passover, unleavened bread, and bitter herbs. Passover, because God passed over the houses of our fathers in Egypt. Unleavened bread because our fathers were redeemed from Egypt. Bitter herbs because the Egyptians embittered the lives of our fathers in Egypt.' In every generation a man must so regard himself as if he came forth himself out of Egypt, for it is written: 'And you shall tell your son in that day saying, "It is because of that which the Lord did for me when I came forth out of Egypt."' Therefore are we bound to give thanks, to praise, to glorify, to honour, to exalt, to extol and to bless him who wrought all these wonders for our fathers and for us. He brought us out from bondage to freedom, from sorrow to gladness, and from mourning to a festival day, and from darkness to great light and from servitude to redemption; so let us say before him the halleluia. [There follows the discussion of the hallel excerpted below.]

After they have mixed for him the third cup he says the benediction over his meal . . . After the Passover meal they should not leave *afikomen*.

(Mishnah *Pesahim* 10.1-5, 7-8)

There are numerous parallels between the rituals regulated by this discussion and those implied by Melito of Sardis in *On Pascha*.[34] Perhaps most interesting is the final statement. The text is virtually untranslatable, and the word *afikomen* has been left untranslated because of disputes over its meaning. However, Daube has suggested that it derives from the Greek *aphikomenos*, 'the one who is to come', and refers to a piece of bread broken off from the main loaf at the beginning of the meal, which is then hidden and brought out of hiding, as a sign of the coming of the Messiah.[35] The similarity to Christian practice is almost too obvious, especially in view of the manner in which Melito hails Christ as the *aphikomenos*. In examining the Mishnaic evidence, however, we should be clear that there is a clear agendum of removing the festival to a domestic setting, and setting up a verbal substitute for the absent lamb. Thus the fourth question, concerning dipping, receives no answer, a phenomenon which comes about, according to Zeitlin, because it originally had reference to dipping into the lamb. Thus the statement of Gamaliel of the things which should be discussed refers to the first three questions, but not to the fourth.[36]

The following discussion on the hallel psalms is found in Mishnah *Pesahim*.

66) How far do they recite the hallel? The school of Shammai say: 'to "A joyful mother of children."' And the school of Hillel say: 'To "A flintstone into a springing well."' ... [Over] a fourth [cup] he completes the hallel and says after it the benediction over song. If he is minded to drink between these cups he may drink; only between the third and the fourth cups he may not drink.

(Mishnah *Pesahim* 10.6)

According to the Mishnah, the hallel Psalms are to be completed at the time of drinking the fourth cup with which the *seder* concludes. Although the disciples are recorded as 'singing a hymn' after the Last Supper, there is no certainty that these psalms are intended. The addition of the fourth cup certainly took place after the parting of the ways, and may have been added to accompany the psalms. Such is clear from the manner in which it is tacked onto the meal, and through the direction that one might not drink between the third and fourth cups (because they follow on directly from one another).[37] However, *Testamentum Domini*, in rewriting *Apostolic Tradition* 25, which refers to the singing of the hallel psalms after supper, locates this ritual on the 'fifth day of the week of Pascha', namely on the day on which the Passover is commemorated in Syrian paschal rites (roughly equating with Maundy Thursday); it is probable that the Syrian redactors were familiar with contemporary Judaism and possible therefore that they recognized the ritual in this light, so incorporating it into Christian practice in their reworking of Hippolytus' text.

---

34 Well summarized by S G Hall, 'Melito in the light of the Passover haggadah' in *JTS* (ns) 22 (1971), pp 29-46.
35 D Daube, *He that cometh* (Diocese of London, 1966).
36 S Zeitlin, 'The liturgy of the first night of Passover' in *JQR* 38 (1947-1948), pp 431-460 at pp 440-443.
37 Thus note the discussion of B Bokser, *The Origins of the Seder* (University of California, Berkeley, 1984), pp 43-4 and references.

Further evidence of mutual influence on paschal rites is provided by the following discussion:

67) How should one roast the Passover offering? 'One should bring a skewer of pomegranate wood and thrust it through from its mouth to its buttocks, laying its legs and its entrails inside it.' The words of R Yosei the Galilean. R Aqiba says that would be of the nature of cooking: but, rather, one should hang them outside it. The Passover offering is roasted neither on a spit nor on a grill. R Zadok said: 'Rabban Gamaliel once said to his slave Tabi: "Go and roast the Passover offering for us on the grill."'

(Mishnah *Pesahim* 7.1-2)

Nodet and Taylor suggest that Gamaliel is trying to avoid the traditional manner of arranging the lamb, which took the shape of a cross, in order to avoid association with Christianity.[21]

Further reading:
Alistair Stewart-Sykes, *The Lamb's High Feast* (Brill, Leiden, 1998)

38   E Nodet and J Taylor, *The Origins of Christianity* (Liturgical Press, Collegeville, 1998), 355.

8
The Sabbath

As is clear from Josephus and Philo (see citations 5-9 above), the fundamental purpose of the Sabbath in early Judaism was study. This aspect of Sabbath observance is found in Syrian and Asian Christianity still in the third and fourth centuries.[39] Although it is possible that this is a borrowing from contemporary Judaism, the extent to which this day is marked by study rather than celebration and refreshment may also be an indication that this is a derivation from the Jewish origins of Christianity in these communities, as in a later period the Sabbath became marked by eating and celebration.

Thus the older tradition is probably that represented here by the practice of R Judah, if not by his justification, according to which eating marks the afternoon before the onset of the Sabbath, a day on which study takes precedence over eating:[40]

> 68) A man should not eat on the eve of the Sabbath from afternoon onwards. 'In order that he should be hungry at the beginning of the Sabbath;'– the words of R Judah.
> Rabban Simeon ben Gamaliel and R Judah and R Yosei were reclining [and eating] in Akko, and the Sabbath began.
> Said Rabban Simeon ben Gamaliel to R Yosei, 'Rabbi, if it is your wish we should stop [eating] because of the [beginning of] Sabbath. He said to him, 'Every day you prefer my opinion to Judah's, and now you prefer Judah's opinion to mine!? "Will you even attack the queen in my presence, in my own house?" (Esther 7.8)'
> Guests were sitting [and eating] with a householder when the Sabbath began, and they got up at nightfall and went to the house of study and returned, and then the cup was mixed for them. 'They recite over it the sanctification of the day': the words of R Judah.
> Rab Yosei says: 'They may continue to eat until it becomes dark.'
> (Tosefta *Berakoth* 5.2-3)

Similarly we may read the following statement by Josephus as indicating that a midday meal was something of a concession:

> 69) . . . in all probability a riot would have ensued, had not the sixth hour arrived and broken up the meeting, for that is the time at which it is lawful for us to eat on the Sabbath. Jonathan and his friends therefore adjourned the council until the following day . . .
> (Josephus, *Life* 279)

---

39   See e g *Apostolic Constitutions* 2.59, *Life of Polycarp* 22, 23, 24.
40   Thus Suetonius, *Augustus* 76.4 speaks of Jews fasting scrupulously on the Sabbath.

70) Rab Eliezer said: 'A man has nothing else to do on a festival except to eat and drink or to sit and study.' Rab Joshua said: 'Divide it, half of it to eating and drinking, and half of it to the house of study.'

(BT *Pesahim* 68B)

Alternative understandings are represented by:

71) R Simon bar Pazzi said in the name of R Joshua bar Levi, in the name of Bar Kapara: 'The one who observes the three meals on the Sabbath shall be preserved from three trials: the sufferings of the messianic age, the final judgement, and the war of Gog and Magog ... The one who observes the Sabbath with joy shall receive an immeasurable inheritance. And what is the manner of observing the Sabbath with joy?' Rab Judah, son of R Samuel bar Shiliath said, in the name of Rab: 'With a meal of beets, big fish and garlic!' Rab Hiyya b Ashi said in Rab's name: 'Even if it is small, if it is prepared in honour of the Sabbath, it is delight. What is it?' Said Rab Papa: 'A pie of fish hash!'

(BT *Shabbath* 118A-B)

72) Our masters have taught us: 'On Friday the sound of the horn should be heard six times. The first to summon the workers from the fields and to cease their labour. The second so that work should stop in the town and the shops close. The third is to kindle the lights. Then there is a pause in the sound for as long as it is necessary to bake a fish or to put bread in the oven, and then it should begin again.'

(BT *Shabbath* 35B)

What is particularly interesting is the prominence of fish in these accounts.[41] That fish should be consumed is particularly interesting, as it may illuminate not only the prominence of fish in the meals reported in the Gospels, but also the statement of Aberkios in the second century that he had fed on fish.[42] Aberkios states that the fish is 'pure food', which may well indicate that special preparation took place before such a meal, such as that undergone by R Judah ben Ilai (see citation 43). In time the meal on the eve of the Sabbath became known in the west as the *cena pura* (pure supper). It is even possible that the significant role played by fish in the diet of the Marcionites derived from this Jewish practice.[43]

The Sabbath was also marked by a special benediction, said over an additional cup.

---

41 Fish is also mentioned as a Jewish food by the Roman satirist Persius at *Satire* 5.179-184. TB Shabbath 119A also records that Raba salted shibute (?mullet) on the eve of the Sabbath, and that Joseph the Sabbath-honourer would always buy fish at market on Sabbath-eve.
42 See the text of Aberkios' epitaph in J B Lightfoot, *The Apostolic Fathers* II.1 (Macmillan, London, 1889), pp 496-497.
43 Eznik, *On God* 407, confirmed by Tertullian, *Against Marcion* 1.14.

73) R Eleazer b Zadok said: 'My father used to say over the cup: "Blessed be he who has sanctified the Sabbath day." He did not add a final benediction.'

(Tosefta *Berakoth* 3.7)

Note also the opinion of R Judah at Tosefta *Berakoth* 5.3 (citation 68 above). Aspects of this blessing are debated in the first century.

74) These are the issues [in dispute] between the house of Shammai and the House of Hillel, concerning the [ritual of the] dinner:

The House of Shammai say, 'One recites the blessing over the day. Then one recites the blessing over the wine. But the House of Hillel say 'First one recites the blessing over the wine, and then one recites the blessing over the day.'

The house of Shammai say, 'First one should wash hands and then mix the cup [of wine].' But the House of Hillel say, 'First one should mix the cup, and then wash the hands.'

The House of Shammai say, 'One should wipe one's hands on the napkin and put it on the table.' But the House of Hillel say, 'On the cushion.'

The House of Shammai say, 'One should sweep the floor [after the meal] and then wash the hands.' [The washing is required before saying the grace after meals]. But the House of Hillel say, 'First one should wash hands, and then sweep the floor.'

The House of Shammai say, 'Lamp, meal, spices, and *habdalah*. [The order of the blessings at the conclusion of the Sabbath] But the House of Hillel says, 'Lamp, spices, meal, and *habdalah*.'

The House of Shammai say, 'Who created the light of the fire.' [At the blessing over the lamp] But the House of Hillel say, 'Who creates the lights of the fire.'

One may not recite a blessing over a lamp or spices of gentiles, nor over a lamp or spices of the dead, nor over a lamp or spices [which have been placed] before [objects pertaining to] idolatry. And one should not recite a blessing over a lamp until one makes use of its light.

(Mishnah *Berakoth* 8)

Several points of interest to students of early Christianity may be noted.

Firstly, that hands are washed before the meal, around the time that the cup is mixed. Box suggests that this is the inspiration for the Johannine footwashing[44], though in this light we should also note the behaviour of R Judah b Elai (citation 44) and, indeed, in view of John's high-priestly typology, the sanctifications of hands and feet undertaken by the high priest.

Secondly, the fact that thanks is given over the cup quite separately from any grace over the meal may illuminate the direction of the ninth chapter of the

---

44 G H Box, 'The Jewish antecedents of the Eucharist' in *JTS* 3 (1902), pp 357-369 at p 362.

Didache that thanks be given first over the cup. This benediction, known as the *qedushah* of the Sabbath, which also occurred on feasts, may thus be the origin of the Didache's eucharistic practice at this point.[45]

Thirdly, the blessing of the lamp and the accompanying ritual may be read in the light of the directions at Hippolytus' *Apostolic Tradition* 25 concerning the entry of the lamp into the community, for which a blessing is said, followed by grace over a cup, followed by grace over a meal. It is to be noted that after the blessing of the lamp, the meal follows the pattern of the Didache's thanksgiving. This opens the question of whether the meal described at this point in *Apostolic Tradition* is an agape, as is generally assumed, particularly since the work of Dix, or itself an ancient witness to the eucharist in a Jewish setting in Rome which has been taken into Hippolytus' work, the redactor perhaps assuming that an agape was meant due to the antiquity of the material with which he was dealing.

Fourthly, the burning of spices after the meal (at least according to the practice of Shammai) may cast light on the report of *Martyrdom of Polycarp* 15 that, apart from smelling of baking bread, the burning body of Polycarp had the scent of burning spices. This report follows the prayer of Polycarp at chapter 14, which is widely regarded as a primitive anaphora. It may also cast light on the prayer for the blessing of spices which follows chapter 9 in the Coptic version of the *Didache*.[46]

Finally it should be observed that the rites of the Sabbath became, like the Passover, essentially domestic as Judaism developed. Thus:

> 75) On account of three transgressions do women die in childbirth: Because they are not meticulous in the laws of menstrual separation, in [those covering] the dough offering, and in [those covering] the kindling of a lamp [for the Sabbath]. Three things should everybody say in his house on the eve of Sabbath, as darkness comes on: 'Have you tithed?' 'Have you prepared the *erub*?' 'Light the lamp!'
>
> (Mishnah *Shabbath* 2.6-7)

Further reading:
S Bacchiocchi, *From Sabbath to Sunday* (Pontifical Gregorian University, Rome, 1977)

---

45 See, as early proponents of this view, G Klein, 'Die Gebete in der Didache' in *ZNW* 9 (1908), pp 132-146, R D Middleton, 'The eucharistic prayers of the Didache' in *JTS* 36 (1935), pp 259-267.
46 Though this is somewhat controversial, as the precise meaning of the term used at this point, as well as the authenticity of this passage, is much debated. See G Buschmann, *Das Martyrium des Polykarp* (Vandenhoek, Göttingen, 1998), pp 307-308 and references.

9
Meals and Graces

Meals in Judaism began with prayer and concluded with graces known as the *birkath haMazon*. It has widely been suggested that these graces are the origin of the eucharist. The following grace-texts are available from the period prior to the parting of the ways.

76) He [Dorotheus] invited Eleazar, 'the oldest of our priests, our guests' to offer a prayer [the setting is a banquet]. He stood and spoke these memorable words 'May the almighty God fill you, O King, with all the blessings which he has created, and may he grant you, your wife, and children, and those of the same mind to enjoy all blessings without end all the days of your life'

(Letter of Aristeas 184-185)

77) And he [Abraham] ate and drank and blessed God most high who created heaven and earth and who made all the fat of the earth and gave it to the children of men so that they might eat and drink and bless their creator. 'And now I give you thanks, my God, because you have let me see this day. Look, I am one hundred and seventy-five years old, old and full of days, and all of my days were peaceful to me. For all the years of my life until this day the sword of the enemy did not triumph over me in anything which you gave to me or to my children. My God, may your mercy and your peace be upon your servant and upon the seed of his sons so that they may be a chosen people for you and an inheritance from all the nations of the earth from henceforth and for all the days of the generations of the earth forever.'

(Jubilees 22.6-9[47])

From these prayers a twofold pattern of thanksgiving (centred on creation, a central theme which also emerges from the brief notice of a grace at *Jubilees* 2.21) and supplication, with an eschatological bent, may be discerned. This is the pattern which is observable in the prayers of the tenth chapter of the Didache, first observed by Klein[48], and frequently thereafter. There is no objection to the existence of a table grace in Greek since this is expressly allowed in the Talmud.

78) The grace after meals: [that this may be recited in any language is derived from] the text, 'And you shall eat and be full, and you shall bless the Lord thy God', in any language in which you say a benediction.

(BT Sotah 33B)

---

47 Jubilees is a retelling of biblical history up to the time of Moses, dating from the second century BCE.
48 G Klein, 'Die Gebete in der Didache' in *ZNW* 9 (1908), pp 132-146; note also R D Middleton, 'The eucharistic prayers of the Didache' in *JTS* 36 (1935), pp 259-267.

We have already observed that the occurrence of the cup before the bread in the Didache's rite may be explained by the occurrence of a festal benediction. The prayer over the bread which follows, and the prayers after the meal may then be explained with reference to these table graces, thus allowing us to trace this aspect of the *Didache*'s practice, like so much else of the *Didache*, to Jewish origins.[49]

In the same context it was observed that *Apostolic Tradition* 25 had the same pattern of a blessing over light, a blessing over a cup and a blessing over bread, as that known to the community of the Didache, and it was suggested that this derived from Jewish practice. The meal described at that point goes on to state that each should say a grace over his own cup. There is no contradiction here with the fact that the bishop has already said grace over a cup, as this is closely reminiscent of the direction in Mishnah *Berakoth*.

> 79) If men sit [apart] to eat, each should say the benediction for himself; if they reclined [around the table together] one should say the benediction for all. If wine is brought to them during the meal each should say the benediction for himself; but if after the meal, one should say the benediction for all, and he, too, should say the benediction over the burning spices even though they are brought in only after the meal is over.
>
> (Mishnah *Berakoth* 6.6)

It would be mistaken to lend a unique validity to the forms of Jewish practice which were taken up by the Tannaim and thus preserved for us in the Mishnah, but here there is a clear parallel which illuminates Christian practice. Nonetheless we should always remember that Judaism before the parting of the ways was a diverse phenomenon. Thus we should also be aware of Essene practice.

> 80) They shall eat in common and bless in common and take counsel in common. Wherever there are ten men to the council of the community they shall not lack a priest among them. And they shall all sit before him according to their rank and shall be asked their counsel in all things in that order. And when the table has been prepared for eating and the new wine for drinking the priest shall be the first to stretch out his hand to bless the first-fruits of the bread and new wine.
>
> (1QS 6.2-6)

> 81) After this purification they assemble in a private apartment which none of the uninitiated is allowed to enter, and as they are now themselves pure they repair to the refectory, as though going to some sacred shrine. They sit down in silence while the baker serves out the loaves to them in order, and the cook sets one plate with a single course before each. The priest says a grace before food, and it is forbidden to partake before the prayer. When breakfast is ended he pronounces a further grace. Thus as day begins and ends they do homage to God as the bountiful giver of life.
>
> (Josephus *Jewish War* 2.129-131)

---

49   Whilst accepting that chapter 10 of the Didache may be explained with reference to these graces, this does not mean that the origin of other eucharistic rites may be explained in the same way.

We may also note the following description of a Jewish group not unlike the Essenes, the Therapeutae, described by Philo.

82) Then they assemble, dressed in white and with faces in which joy is mingled with the utmost seriousness. Before they recline at a signal from the member of the rota, for this is the name given to those who serve in this way among them, they stand straight and in order and lift up their eyes and hands to heaven. Their eyes, because they are trained to fix their gaze on things worthy of contemplation, their hands to signify that they are pure from taking gain, and that they are not polluted by the making of profit. So they stand and pray that their feast might be acceptable to God and that they might act in accordance with his will.

(Philo *On the contemplative life* 66)

One may, moreover, note (although its Essene origin is not assured):

83) . . . [. . .] to be comforted during her mourning. Her misery [. . .] to de[st]roy peoples and he will uproot nations and the wicked [. . .] ?Renew the works of the heavens and of the earth, and they shall rejoice and [all the earth shall be] filled with his glory. He will atone [for] their [guilt] and the one who is great in goodness will comfort them. ?The [. . .] is good so to eat its fruit and its goodness [. . .] As somebody whom his mother comforts so I shall comfort them in Jerusal[em . . . Like a bridegroom] with his bride he shall live for all [ag]es. His throne is everlasting without end and his glory [. . .] and all peoples. [. . .] and there shall be within it . . . [. . .] and their [e]arth desirable. [. . .] beaut[y . . .] I will bless. [. . .] Blessed be the name of the most high [. . .] your mercy on me. [. . .] for the law which you have established [. . .] ?your book of your laws . . .

(4Q 434a)

Here there is a strong eschatological element.[50]

84) How is the communal grace introduced? In a company of three one says: 'Let us bless'. In a company of three besides oneself one says 'Bless!'[Imperative]. In a company of ten one says: 'Let us bless the Lord our God'. In a company of a hundred besides oneself: 'Bless the Lord our God.' In a company of a thousand one says: 'Let us bless the Lord our God, the God of Israel.' In a company of a thousand besides oneself one says: 'Bless!' In a company of ten thousand besides himself he says: 'Bless!' In the manner in which he utters the benediction, so they answer after him: 'Blessed be the Lord our God, the God of Israel, the God of hosts who sits between the Cherubim, for the food which we have eaten.' R Yosei the Galilean says: 'They utter the benediction in accordance with the size of the gathering (*qahal*), as it is said: "Bless God in congregations (*qehaloth*), even the Lord, from the fountain of Israel."' R Aqiba said: 'What do we find in the synagogue (*beit haKnesset*)? Whether there be many or few, one says: "Bless the Lord."' R Ishmael says: 'Bless the Lord who is to be blessed.'

(Mishnah *Berakoth* 7.3)

---

50   For a discussion of this fragment see M Weinfeld, 'Grace after meals at Qumran' in *JBL* 111 (1992), pp 427-440.

The point of interest here is that the formulae are different from those generally known in that they are not pure *berakah* form; the divergence from the usage of the synagogue which R Aqiba observes is also significant, as it points to divergence between domestic meal practice and that of the school. This indicates that the formularies are survivals from earlier practices in *haburah* meals.[51] However, in discussing the relationship between the *birkath haMazon* and the eucharist, scholars generally have reference to the forms exhibited in the Babylonian Talmud, during which period the forms are moving towards standardization, and as a result have developed since the parting of the ways.

85) Our rabbis taught: 'The order of grace after meals is as follows. The first benediction is that of "Who feeds". The second is the benediction of the land. The third is "Who builds Jerusalem." The fourth is "Who is good and bestows good."'

(BT *Berakoth* 48B)

It should be noted that even here there is some debate concerning the precise wording of the benedictions.

In our examination of the earlier forms, it was observed that there was little emphasis on blessing, but that thanksgiving was more prominent. In this way there is greater conformity with the *Didache*. Thus, on the basis of later literary forms of these blessings, Talley asks the question of how *berakoth* were transmuted into thanksgivings addressed directly to God, and as part of his answer suggests that the Didache transposes the first two sections of the *birkath haMazon*.[52] When he does this, he makes a fluid liturgical practice behave like a written text, and then attributes to the community of the Didache literary activity on a text which never existed. It is, moreover, an attempt to answer an unnecessary question, because the emphasis on thanksgiving in the earlier examples, and the absence of a pure *berakah* form in the pre-Mishnaic period, mean that a transition from thanksgiving to blessing was never necessary! Rather there has been a transition from thanksgiving to blessing in rabbinic Judaism.

The extent of variety which might be exhibited in the forms may, moreover, be illustrated by the following text from the second or third century:[53]

86) Blessed be the Lord, King of the Universe who created all things, apportioned food, appointed drink for all the children of flesh with which they shall be satisfied. To us human beings, he granted to partake of the food of the myriads of his <?angelic bodies> For all this we are bound to bless with songs (selah) in gatherings . . ..

---

51 So J Heinemann, 'Birkath ha-zimmun and havurah meals' in *JJS* 13 (1962), pp 23-29.
52 T J Talley, 'From *berakah* to *eucharistia*: a re-opening question' in *Worship* 50 (1976), pp 115-137.
53 The reconstruction of the fragment follows the rather speculative reconstruction of J L Teicher, 'Ancient eucharistic prayers in Hebrew' in *JQR* (1963-1964), pp 99-109.

[*a lacuna follows*]
    to praise (?) his (?greatness)
    sustains (?)
    great(?) and small animals
    all the beasts of the field
    food for the birds (?of the sky)
    (clothed) him in skin and flesh

(Dura Europos parchment D 25)

Teicher thinks that this is a Hebrew eucharistic prayer. However the mention of angelic bodies is entirely Teicher's reconstruction and has no textual support. The fragment is therefore just as likely to be Jewish, a version of the *birkath haMazon*. It just about possible that it is a tract from a butcher's shop! Positively it demonstrates the prominence of the theme of creation in Jewish thanksgivings, as well as its variety.

Nonetheless it is possible that one Talmudic usage, despite its chronological distance from the first century, might illuminate one early Christian usage:

87) One should not say the blessing at the breaking of the bread for guests, unless one eats with them.

(BT *Rosh Hashanah* 29B)

Since this is a reference to the thanksgiving at the beginning of the meal, it remains probable that these prayers were the origin of some Christian eucharistic rites.

Further reading:
Enrico Mazza, *The origins of the eucharistic prayer* (Liturgical Press, Collegeville, 1995)

Appendix: Index of passages

THE GROUP FOR RENEWAL OF WORSHIP (GROW)

This Group, originally founded in 1961, has for thirty years taken responsibility for the Grove Books publications on liturgy and worship. Its membership and broad aims reflect a highly reforming, pastoral and missionary interest in worship. Beginning with a youthful evangelical Anglican membership in the early 1970s, the Group has not only probed adventurously into the future of Anglican worship, but has also with growing sureness of touch taken its place in promoting weighty scholarship. Thus the list of 'Grove Liturgical Studies' (on page 47) shows how, over a twelve-year period, the quarterly Studies added steadily to the material available to students of patristic, reformation and modern scholarly issues in liturgy. In 1986 the Group was approached by the Alcuin Club Committee with a view to publishing the new series of Joint Liturgical Studies, and this series is, at the time of writing, in its fifteenth year of publication, sustaining the programme with three Studies each year.

Between the old Grove Liturgical Studies and the new Joint Liturgical Studies there is a large provision of both English language texts and other theological works on the patristic era. A detailed consolidated list is available from the publishers.

Since the early 1970s the Group has had Colin Buchanan as chairman and Trevor Lloyd as vice-chairman.

THE ALCUIN CLUB

The Alcuin Club exists to promote the study of Christian liturgy in general, and in particular the liturgies of the Anglican Communion. Since its foundation in 1897 it has published over 130 books and pamphlets. Members of the Club receive some publications of the current year free and others at a reduced rate.

Information concerning the annual subscription, applications for membership and lists of publications is obtainable from the Treasurer, The Revd. T. R. Barker, The Parsonage, 8 Church Street, Spalding, Lincs. PE11 2 PB. (Tel. 01775 722675).

The Alcuin Club has worked with a number of publishers in the UK and the USA to publish a major work of liturgical scholarship every year. Recent books include *Make Music to Our God* (Reginald Box SSF), *The Rites of Christian Initiation: Their Evolution and Interpretation* (Maxwell Johnson), *Daily Prayer in Christian Spain: A Study of the Mazarabic Office* (Graham Woolfenden) and *A Companion to Common Worship, volumne 1* (edited by Paul Bradsahw).

In 2002, Alcuin and SPCK will publish two Liturgical Guides—on art and worship (Christopher Irvine and Anne Dawtry) and memorial services (Donald Gray).

The Alcuin Club's annual subscription entitles members to receive, without further charge, the three Joint Liturgical Studies and the Club's major annual publication. Occasionally, further books are offered to members at discounted prices.

Alcuin/GROW Joint Liturgical Studies

All cost £4.95 (US $8) in 2001—nos. 4 and 16 are out of print

1. **(LS 49) Daily and Weekly Worship—from Jewish to Christian** by Roger Beckwith
2. **(LS 50) The Canons of Hippolytus** edited by Paul Bradshaw
3. **(LS 51) Modern Anglican Ordination Rites** edited by Colin Buchanan
4. **(LS 52) Models of Liturgical Theology** by James Empereur
5. **(LS 53) A Kingdom of Priests: Liturgical Formation of the Laity: The Brixen Essays** edited by Thomas Talley
6. **(LS 54) The Bishop in Liturgy: an Anglican Study** edited by Colin Buchanan
7. **(LS 55) Inculturation: the Eucharist in Africa** by Phillip Tovey
8. **(LS 56) Essays in Early Eastern Initiation** edited by Paul Bradshaw,
9. **(LS 57) The Liturgy of the Church in Jerusalem** by John Baldovin
10. **(LS 58) Adult Initiation** edited by Donald Withey
11. **(LS 59) 'The Missing Oblation': The Contents of the Early Antiochene Anaphora** by John Fenwick
12. **(LS 60) Calvin and Bullinger on the Lord's Supper** by Paul Rorem
13-14 **(LS 61) The Liturgical Portions of the Apostolic Constitutions: A Text for Students** edited by W. Jardine Grisbrooke (This double-size volume costs double price (i.e. £9.90))
15 **(LS 62) Liturgical Inculturation in the Anglican Communion** edited by David Holeton
16. **(LS 63) Cremation Today and Tomorrow** by Douglas Davies
17. **(LS 64) The Preaching Service—The Glory of the Methodists** by Adrian Burdon
18. **(LS 65) Irenaeus of Lyon on Baptism and Eucharist** edited with Introduction, Translation and Commentary by David Power
19. **(LS 66) Testamentum Domini** edited by Grant Sperry-White
20. **(LS 67) The Origins of the Roman Rite** edited by Gordon Jeanes
21. **The Anglican Eucharist in New Zealand 1814-1989** by Bosco Peters
22-23 **Foundations of Christian Music: The Music of Pre-Constantinian Christianity** by Edward Foley (double-sized volume at £9.90)
24. **Liturgical Presidency** by Paul James
25. **The Sacramentary of Sarapion of Thmuis: A Text for Students** edited by Ric Lennard-Barrett
26. **Communion Outside the Eucharist** by Phillip Tovey
27. **Revising the Eucharist: Groundwork for the Anglican Communion** edited by David Holeton
28. **Anglican Liturgical Inculturation in Africa** edited by David Gitari
29-30. **On Baptismal Fonts: Ancient and Modern** by Anita Stauffer (double-sized volume at £9.90)
31. **The Comparative Liturgy of Anton Baumstark** by Fritz West
32. **Worship and Evangelism in Pre-Christendom** by Alan Kreider
33. **Liturgy in Early Christian Egypt** by Maxwell E. Johnson
34. **Welcoming the Baptized** by Timothy Turner
35. **Daily Prayer in the Reformed Tradition: An Initial Survey** by Diane Karay Tripp
36. **The Ritual Kiss in Early Christian Worship** by Edward Phillips
37. **'After the Primitive Christians': The Eighteenth-century Anglican Eucharist in its Architectural Setting** by Peter Doll
38. **Coronations Past, Present and Future** edited by Paul Bradshaw
39. **Anglican Orders and Ordinations** edited by David Holeton
40. **The Liturgy of St James as presently used** edited by Phillip Tovey
41. **Anglican Missals** by Mark Dalby
42. **The Origins of the Roman Rite vol 2** edited by Gordon Jeanes
43. **Baptism in Early Byzantine Palestine 325-451** by Juliette Day
44. **Ambrosianum Mysterium: the Church of Milan and its Liturgical Tradition Vol. 1** by Cesare Alzati (translated by George Guiver)
45. **Mar Nestorius and Mar Theodore the Interpreter: the Forgotten Eucharistic Prayers of East Syria** edited by Bryan Spinks
46. **The Eucharistic Theology of the Later Nonjurors** by James Smith
47-48. **Ambrosianum Mysterium: the Church of Milan and its Liturgical Tradition Vol. II** by Cesare Alzati (translated by George Guiver) (double-sized volume at £9.90)
49. **The Syriac Version of the Liturgy of St James: A brief history for Students** by Dr Baby Varghese
50. **Offerings from Kenya to Anglicanism: Liturgical Texts and Contents including 'A Kenyan Service of Holy Communion'** by Graham Kings and Geoff Morgan
51. **Early Jewish Liturgy: A Source Book for use by Students of Eearly Christian Liturgy** edited and translated by Alistair Stewart-Sykes and Judith H Newman

Grove Liturgical Studies

This series began in March 1975, and was published quarterly until 1986. Each title has 32 or 40 pages. No's 1, 3-6, 9, 10, 16, 30, 33, 36, 44 and 46 are out of print. Asterisked numbers have been reprinted. Prices in 2001. £2.75.